LUST FOR SHOES

A POSTCARD BOOK™

Running Press
Philadelphia, Pennsylvania

Postcard Book is a trademark of Running Press Book Publishers.

Canadian representatives: General Publishing Co., Ltd., 30 Lesmill Road, Don Mills, Ontario M3B 2T6. International representatives: Worldwide Media Services, Inc., 115 East Twenty-third Street, New York, New York 10010.

9   8   7   6   5   4   3   2
The digit on the right indicates the number of this printing.

ISBN 0–89471–821–5

Cover design by Toby Schmidt
Interior design by Eric Walker
Typography by Commcor Communications Corporation, Philadelphia, Pennsylvania
Printed and bound in the United States of America by Innovation Printing

This book may be ordered by mail from the publisher. Please add $2.50 for postage and handling for each copy. *But try your bookstore first!* Running Press Book Publishers, 125 South Twenty-second Street, Philadelphia, Pennsylvania 19103.

LUST for SHOES

A POSTCARD BOOK™

AMERICAN
POSTCARD

Running Press Book Publishers

LUST FOR SHOES
A POSTCARD BOOK™

AMERICAN
POSTCARD

1276
POSTMODERN POSTCARDS
151 FIRST AVE #150
NYC 10003

Running Press Book Publishers

LUST FOR SHOES

A POSTCARD BOOK™

AMERICAN
POSTCARD

Running Press Book Publishers

LUST for SHOES

A POSTCARD BOOK™

AMERICAN
POSTCARD

Running Press Book Publishers

LUST FOR SHOES
A POSTCARD BOOK™

AMERICAN
POSTCARD

1288
POSTMODERN POSTCARDS
151 FIRST AVE #150
NYC 10003

Running Press Book Publishers

LUST FOR SHOES

A POSTCARD BOOK™

AMERICAN
POSTCARD

Running Press Book Publishers

LUST FOR SHOES

A POSTCARD BOOK™

AMERICAN
POSTCARD

Running Press Book Publishers

LUST FOR SHOES

A POSTCARD BOOK™

AMERICAN
POSTCARD

Running Press Book Publishers

YOU'VE WON!!
CONGRATULATIONS!
WATCH FOR DELIVERY OF YOUR FREE GIFT!!

LUST**for**SHOES

A POSTCARD BOOK™

AMERICAN
POSTCARD

1262
© THE AMERICAN POSTCARD CO., INC., NEW YORK
PHOTOGRAPH: PETRIFIED FILM ARCHIVES
ALL RIGHTS RESERVED

Running Press Book Publishers

LUST FOR SHOES

A POSTCARD BOOK™

AMERICAN
POSTCARD

Running Press Book Publishers

LUST FOR SHOES

A POSTCARD BOOK™

AMERICAN
POSTCARD

Running Press Book Publishers

LUST FOR SHOES

A POSTCARD BOOK™

AMERICAN
POSTCARD

1247
© THE AMERICAN POSTCARD CO., INC., NEW YORK
PHOTOGRAPH: PETRIFIED FILM ARCHIVES
ALL RIGHTS RESERVED

Running Press Book Publishers

LUST FOR SHOES

A POSTCARD BOOK™

AMERICAN
POSTCARD

Running Press Book Publishers

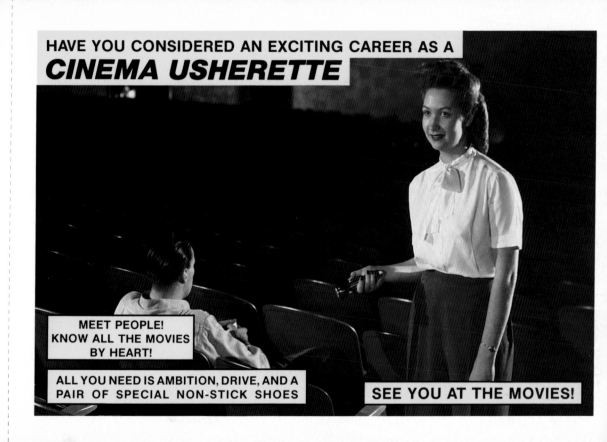

LUST FOR SHOES
A POSTCARD BOOK™

AMERICAN
POSTCARD

Running Press Book Publishers

LUST FOR SHOES

A POSTCARD BOOK™

AMERICAN
POSTCARD

Running Press Book Publishers

LUST FOR SHOES

A POSTCARD BOOK™

AMERICAN
POSTCARD

Running Press Book Publishers

LUST FOR SHOES

A POSTCARD BOOK™

AMERICAN
POSTCARD

Running Press Book Publishers

LUSTꜰᴏʀSHOES

A POSTCARD BOOK™

1090
© THE AMERICAN POSTCARD CO., INC., NEW YORK
PHOTOGRAPH: PETRIFIED FILM ARCHIVES

AMERICAN
POSTCARD

Running Press Book Publishers

LUST FOR SHOES

A POSTCARD BOOK™

AMERICAN POSTCARD

1293
POSTMODERN POSTCARDS
151 FIRST AVE #150
NYC 10003

Running Press Book Publishers

LUST FOR SHOES

A POSTCARD BOOK™

AMERICAN
POSTCARD

Running Press Book Publishers

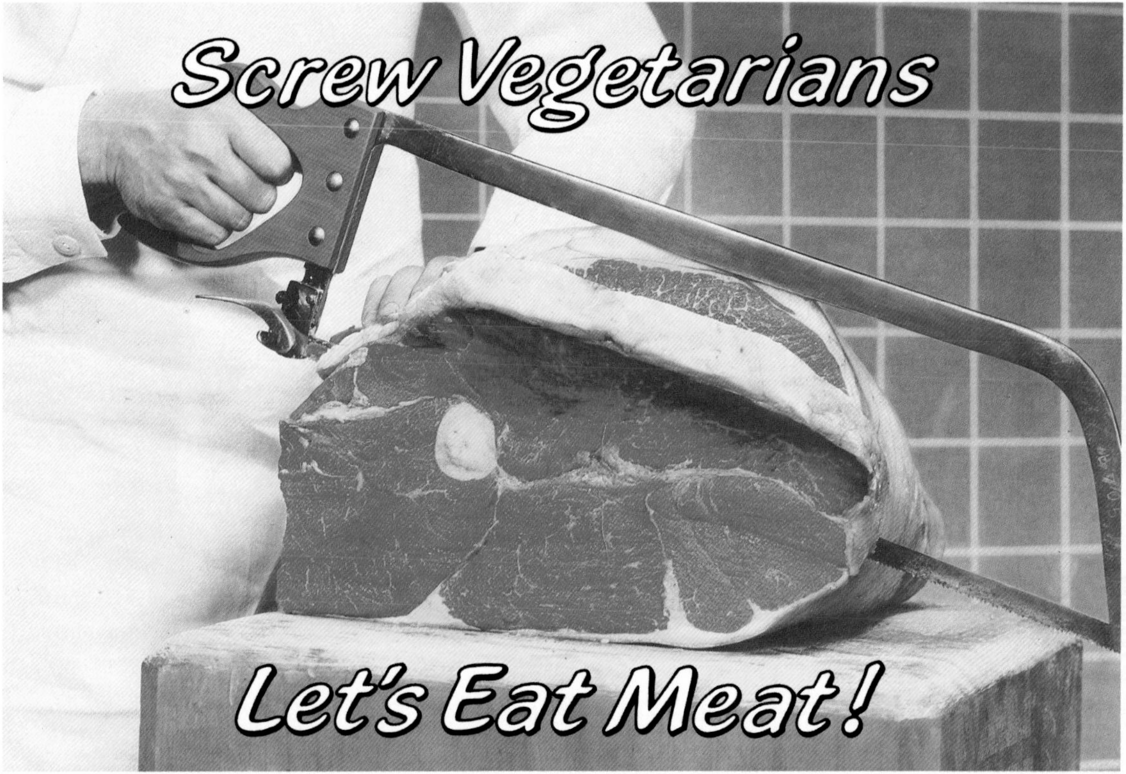
Screw Vegetarians
Let's Eat Meat!

LUST FOR SHOES

A POSTCARD BOOK™

AMERICAN
POSTCARD

1251
POSTMODERN POSTCARDS
151 FIRST AVE #150
NYC 10003

Running Press Book Publishers

LUST**FOR**SHOES

A POSTCARD BOOK™

AMERICAN
POSTCARD

1277
POSTMODERN POSTCARDS
151 FIRST AVE #150
NYC 10003

Running Press Book Publishers

We're Praying For Your Salvation

LUST FOR SHOES

A POSTCARD BOOK™

AMERICAN
POSTCARD

Running Press Book Publishers

LUST FOR SHOES

A POSTCARD BOOK™

AMERICAN POSTCARD

1279
POSTMODERN POSTCARDS
151 FIRST AVE #150
NYC 10003

Running Press Book Publishers

LUST**FOR**SHOES

A POSTCARD BOOK™

AMERICAN
POSTCARD

1282
POSTMODERN POSTCARDS
151 FIRST AVE #150
NYC 10003

Running Press Book Publishers

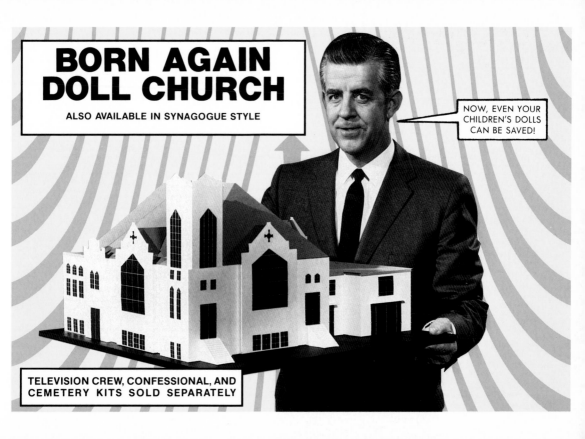

LUST FOR SHOES

A POSTCARD BOOK™

AMERICAN POSTCARD

1285
POSTMODERN POSTCARDS
151 FIRST AVE #150
NYC 10003

Running Press Book Publishers

LUST FOR SHOES
A POSTCARD BOOK™

AMERICAN
POSTCARD

1289
POSTMODERN POSTCARDS
151 FIRST AVE #150
NYC 10003

Running Press Book Publishers

LUST FOR SHOES

A POSTCARD BOOK™

AMERICAN
POSTCARD

1286
POSTMODERN POSTCARDS
151 FIRST AVE #150
NYC 10003

Running Press Book Publishers

LUST FOR SHOES

A POSTCARD BOOK™

AMERICAN
POSTCARD

1270
© THE AMERICAN POSTCARD CO., INC., NEW YORK
PHOTOGRAPH: PETRIFIED FILM ARCHIVES

Running Press Book Publishers

WELL, THIS ABOUT SUMS UP EVERYTHING I KNOW

LUST FOR SHOES

A POSTCARD BOOK™

AMERICAN
POSTCARD

Running Press Book Publishers